RIVERS
OF AMERICA

RIVERS
OF AMERICA

GALLERY BOOKS
an imprint of W.H. Smith Publishers, Inc.,
112 Madison Avenue
New York, New York 10016

To Kirsten and Adam

PAGE ONE:

Many bridges span a reddened Ohio River. Barges plying Kentucky's 660 miles of Ohio River carry nearly as much cargo as the Panama Canal.

PAGE THREE:

Two canoeists are silhouetted against the gold-plated waters of the Nahanni River, Northwest Territories.

PAGE FIVE:

Two white-water rafters are tossed along the Colorado River beneath the Grand Canyon, Arizona.

Published in Canada by Discovery Books

First published in the United States in 1991 by Gallery Books, an imprint of W.H. Smith Publishers Inc., 112 Madison Avenue, New York, New York 10016

ISBN 0 8317 7400 2

Typesetting: Imprint Typesetting
Printed and bound in Hong Kong

C O N T E N T S

COLE'S HILL

1

HISTORIC RIVERS

IMAGINE SETTING OUT ON A VOYAGE WITH ONLY THE VAGUEST notion where you are going, without any map or chart to show you the way, with a cache of supplies you have no way of knowing will be sufficient to sustain you on the way there, much less on the way back.

It is a foolish traveler who will embark on a journey under such conditions.

But fine is the line between foolishness and daring, and it was under precisely these conditions that Jacques Cartier loosed the lines and sailed from the Old World in 1534 in search of the fortunes of the Orient. We can only imagine his dismay when he and his crew encountered the brooding brow of North America looming before them—a landscape of scrubby trees and fists of rock and clouds of infuriating insects. No wonder Cartier turned to his journal and sighed: "I am inclined to think that this must be the land which God gave as his portion to Cain."

Plymouth Rock as seen from Cole's Hill, Massachusetts.

It is a measure of the lure of Cathay that Cartier and other early explorers did not simply curse their luck and turn for home but pressed inland, often to their intense discomfort and pain and sometimes to their deaths.

To say such explorers were a hardy breed is to understate by a broad margin. They set out in boats not much larger than the recreational craft which litter the rivers and lakes of twentieth century North America. They endured tempests which would keep a modern-day Sunday sailor snug and thankful at berth in a marina. And their crews were often overworked and underfed; it was a rare captain who did not preside at a service which ended with the body of a sailor sliding into the sea.

Skirting Giovani Caboto's New Founde Lande, Cartier found an even more formidable obstacle: a massive shore stretching as far as he could see both south and north. With no evident route around it, Cartier sought a river which might take him through the land mass to Cathay. He came close. Nosing about in what is now known as the Gulf of St. Lawrence, Cartier became the first European to chart the shores of a gulf that would lead to lakes and distant rivers and would twist, in turn, into the very heart of a new land.

By October of the following year, Cartier had explored as far upriver as Hochelaga—now Montreal—and discovered the rapids which served as a barrier to the interior for all but the smallest and most portable craft—the canoe. Nothing, however, was to prepare him for the brutality of a North American winter. Lodged months later in Stadacona, our present day Quebec, Cartier and his men were caught suddenly and unexpectedly in the grip of winter and their ships held fast in the lock of the river's grinding ice.

Nearly seventy years would pass before the next important European explorations. Then, almost simultaneously, two of the most famed of the travelers would find themselves probing the interior of this new land within several hundred miles of each other.

In the summer of 1609, Henry Hudson began charting the lands of what is now New York State. Having temporarily given up hope of finding a north west passage, and granted a commission from the Dutch East India Company, Hudson set out to explore and lay claim to whatever likely lands he came across. He encountered, along the Hudson River route, lush vegetation and pristine banks, a bucolic contrast to the stark Arctic shores he had been exploring the previous few years. No doubt he wished the following year, adrift and freezing to death with his son and a few faithful crew, that he had made a clearing for himself in the forests along the Hudson River rather than embarking on the fateful final voyage in the bay which would bear his name and become his grave.

While Hudson was probing the upper reaches of the river further south, Samuel de Champlain and his crew of twenty-eight were exploring North American waters further north. Champlain had been intrigued by a number of these rivers—he had stumbled upon, and named, the Saint John while probing the Bay of Fundy—but it was the St. Lawrence which captured his imagination. Spending the summer and winter of 1608 in trying to achieve a French toehold at a promontory the Indian people called "the narrows", Champlain and his crew began constructing "The Habitation of Quebec"—the first permanent European settlement along the shores of the St. Lawrence. It appeared a perfect place for such a colony. From the heights, Champlain could look down the broad sweep of river leading to the sea, and could gaze upstream toward

In New York State, Quebec or Ontario, land on both sides of the St. Lawrence River is lush and used principally for agriculture.

the heart of the land which would provide him, and his patrons, a fortune in furs. He was building alongside the first major highway in North America. For Champlain, and for hundreds who followed him, it was simply that: an avenue into the heart of the fur-trapping lands, leading out again to the markets of Europe.

The construction of this primitive settlement—a few log buildings, surrounded by mud—was achieved at considerable cost. By the spring of 1609, Champlain had buried twenty of his men, all of whom had fallen victim to scurvy and the cold.

The following year, a French teenager named Etienne Brûlé left Champlain's new settlement of Quebec and made his way inland. Brûlé was bound for the country around Georgian Bay, his goal to live among the Huron people. Brûlé was the first of a breed of independent-headed young men who, known as *coureurs de bois*, would open up the heart of North America to trade. During the next decade, Brûlé traveled widely with the roving Hurons and is thought to be the first European explorer to canoe down the swift-running and then nameless rivers which rushed into lakes Ontario, Erie, Huron and Superior.

The tale is romantic: pushing through the bush and propelled along turbulent waters, Brûlé would have been rewarded with spectacular vistas, each unpredictable in turn. The reality was something else again. These were treacherous lands, and the Hurons had hundreds of equally treacherous enemies. More than a few Hurons, and their European allies, paid for a moment's inattention with their lives. The rivers, furthermore, down which these people paddled in search of furs, were anything but peaceful streams. Rounding a bend, the careless voyageur could find himself in the grip of currents which would sweep him helpless over a cataract to his death.

From spring through autumn, travelers in the woods were besieged by swarms of insects, and had to keep a constant watch for much larger, and more dangerous, enemies in the form of bears, lynx and wolves.

The French were not alone in their desire to take advantage of this new land. In the summer of 1619, Danish explorer Jens Munck skirted icebergs and treeless shores, and made his way into Hudson Bay. All around were astonishing signs of wildlife: whales, walrus, seals and a host of birds he could not have seen anywhere else on earth. Munck also discovered, as Hudson had before him, that winter waits for no man. Although Munck and his men found relative safety near the mouth of the Churchill River, the landscape must have appeared to be the very end of the world. So cold was it, and so blistering the winds, that a man's flesh might freeze in a matter of seconds. Were he to wander out into a storm, only blind luck would lead him back to a flapping tent, death awaiting those who were lost outside.

By the time the ice started melting the following spring, the cold had claimed sixty-one of Munck's men. Amazingly, their ships survived, and in the summer of 1620, Munck and his fellow explorers picked their way between the majestic silver and aqua floes of Hudson Bay to open water and, eventually, to their homes.

Two of the most famous explorers of the New World were Louis Jolliet and Father Jacques Marquette who, together in 1672, were sent by Quebec intendent Jean Talon to explore the Mississippi River. No one then knew whether the river emptied into the Pacific—thus constituting the fabled passage to

Cathay—or flowed directly south to the Gulf of Mexico. By the following summer, Jolliet and Marquette managed to navigate the Mississippi as far south as the confluence with the Arkansas River. They were, in fact, the first Europeans to witness the incredible diversity of this magnificent river. From its rushing upper reaches, coursing through northern mountains and forests, to its lazy lower extremities where its muddy face appears as calm as a creek, the Mississippi remains a difficult and inconstant river.

Jolliet and Marquette were lucky to survive their introduction to the Missouri where it plunges into the Mississippi. Finding the confluence of these two rivers "a frightening outpouring", the two explorers were forced to dodge tree trunks and other debris being swept into the Mississippi. Although they succeeded in discovering the Missouri and in tracing the Mississippi farther south than any European explorers thus far, their success proved bad news for Talon. Jolliet and Marquette had traveled far enough by the time they reached the Arkansas to rule out the possibility that the Mississippi might turn west and provide access to the Pacific and, eventually, to the legendary wealth of the Orient.

It was left to the mentally-unstable René-Robert Cavelier de La Salle to follow the Mississippi to its mouth in the Gulf. A proven liar, a known schemer and a man filled with visions of personal grandeur, La Salle is justly famous for his travels down the Mississippi River in 1682—a feat which permitted Louis XIV of France to claim Louisiana as his own.

Born in France in 1643, La Salle set out to join the Society of Jesus. The Jesuits released him from his vows when they learned just how unstable a character they had allowed in their midst. Undaunted, La Salle made his way across the Atlantic to the New World, undertook explorations with Sulpician priests—during which time he came across the Ohio River—and in 1673 fell in with supporters of Governor General Louis de Buade, Comte de Frontenac. La Salle somehow managed to implore Frontenac to procure him letters of nobility. Five years later, he set out to establish a chain of forts in what is now the American mid-west.

La Salle and a crew of supporters had the distinction of building, launching and manning the first ship to sail the Great Lakes. The barque *Griffon* was built on the banks of Cayuga Creek, a tributary of the Niagara River, and in the summer of 1679 navigated Lake Erie, the Detroit River, Lake St. Clair, the St. Clair River and Lake Huron all the way to Michilimackinac and Green Bay. Eventually, the Griffon was lost in a storm, most probably in Lake Michigan, while en route back to the Niagara with a load of furs. La Salle was not on board at the time.

For those who wanted to move into this new territory, La Salle and his followers had broken the trail. They established trading posts, and settlements grew up rapidly around them. Although La Salle did not live long enough to see the fruits of his labors—he was murdered by his men in 1687—these little settlements have now flourished and grown into full-fledged cities and towns.

The late seventeenth and the early eighteenth centuries were active times for those in search of adventure and lands to claim for their countries. Henry Kelsey, on behalf of the Hudson Bay Company, undertook a number of explorations in what is now western Canada and in 1690 discovered the fourth largest river system in Canada—the Saskatchewan. Its two branches—the north which passes through Edmonton and Prince Albert, and the south which cuts through Calgary, Medicine Hat and Saskatoon— have a combined length of more than 2,300 miles.

The La Verendrye brothers, Louis-Joseph and François, went on to explore the Saskatchewan to its headwaters during their epic explorations in the 1740s.

The North Saskatchewan is born in the Columbia Icefields and rushes out of the mountains, past present-day Edmonton and across the prairies, cutting deep valleys as it goes and taking soil and sediment with it on its journey to Lake Winnipeg. The South Saskatchewan is formed by the joining of the Oldman and Bow rivers and runs parallel to its northern sister, eventually joining it. Both rivers were perhaps best described by the Indian people who gave them their present name, Kisiskatchewani: translated into "swift-flowing river."

In one fifteen-month period, the La Verendrye brothers made their way down the Missouri and overland to the Yellowstone River, turned south and then west circling back to the Missouri—all in search of the fabled gulf which was thought to lie somewhere in the west and drain into the Pacific Ocean. They found no western sea, but they did get as far as the mountains of Wyoming.

Much farther north, in a brief period about thirty years later, several adventurers succeeded in exploring and mapping much of the wilderness which is now Canada's north. The most remarkable exploration was the journey by foot, from the western shore of Hudson Bay to the Coronation Gulf in the Arctic, that spanned more than two thousand miles and was fueled by the vision of a mysterious northern river and a wealth of copper glittering in the sun.

The journey was made by a timid Englishman named Samuel Hearne. Hearne had been stationed at the Hudson Bay Company outpost at Prince of Wales Fort on Hudson Bay. There, he met some Indians who had come to trade copper. When Hearne asked where they had found the metal, they replied vaguely that they had unearthed it near the mouth of a great river far to the north and west.

Hearne determined to go to the site himself, full of hope that it would lead to riches for his employer, and enhanced status for himself. He, a Chipewyan guide named Matonabbee and a party of Matonabbee's followers set out in December 1770 and wandered for more than a year before coming across the northern-flowing Coppermine, following it to its outlet at the Arctic Ocean. Scour the area though he did, Hearne succeeded in finding only one piece of copper.

It was adjacent to the mouth of the Coppermine that Matonabbee and his companions encountered a band of Inuit—their traditional enemy—and promptly engaged in a slaughter at a site which Hearne named Bloody Fall. Though they demanded that he help them, Hearne refused, and having lost their confidence and friendship, Hearne could barely keep up with his guides as they hurried south. In June of 1772, the party arrived back at Prince of Wales Fort, eighteen months after they had set out.

Hearne considered the journey a total failure. The Coppermine was useless as a trade route, and it led to no minerals which would enrich either his company or himself. He retired to England, fifteen years after his Copper-

OPPOSITE PAGE:

Multnomah Falls, Oregon, in the Columbia River Gorge after a February snowfall.

mine journey, and spent the last years of his life writing a chronicle of his exploits. He died in 1792, three years before the book was to be published and would bring him fame.

Twenty years after Hearne's epic travels across the north, another explorer—much more respected and successful in his own time—was about to set out on another unprecedented journey.

Alexander Mackenzie was a boy of fifteen when, in 1779, he signed on with a fur-trading company in Montreal and five years later was made a partner. When the outfit merged with the North West Company, Mackenzie became a founding partner. He was twenty-three. Assigned to the North West Company's post on the Athabasca, Mackenzie became fired with the ambition to map out what is now known as the Mackenzie River basin in the hope of discovering the Pacific and hence a route to Cathay. Following the Mackenzie River to its outlet became for Alexander Mackenzie the "favorite project of my own ambition."

Mackenzie pursued the river only to find that it led not to the Pacific, but to the Arctic, and that its outlet was the Beaufort Sea. Retracing his steps in 1793, Mackenzie set out on the Slave River, traveling south to Lake Athabasca where he turned to follow the Peace River, and crossing a river route which he would name in honor of his fellow North West Company partner, Simon Fraser. Mackenzie was all for following the Fraser to its outlet, but his Indian companions persuaded him instead to travel overland where he crossed the Continental divide, picked up the Bella Coola River and followed it to the Pacific. These two remarkable journeys—spanning what is now Canada's Northwest Territories, from south to north, and Alberta and British Columbia, from east to west—established his fame.

More than half a century would pass between the La Verendrye brothers' 1740s exploration of the Missouri and the first successful navigation of its length. Meriwether Lewis and William Clark embarked on the Missouri in 1804. They managed to navigate, or portage, the river's entire length: no mean feat since the river measures 2,714 miles from the point where it rages into the Mississippi to the point where it is born in western Montana at the confluence of the Jefferson, Madison and Gallatin rivers. Not content with finding the river's source, Lewis and Clark crossed the Rocky Mountains and descended the Columbia River to the Pacific. They then retraced their route down the "Big Muddy" to the Mississippi—all in the space of two years. It ranks even now as one of the greatest adventures in North American history.

More than a quarter century later, Henry Rowe Schoolcraft ascended the Mississippi all the way to northern Minnesota and identified Lake Itasca as the source of "The Father of Waters." By the time he did so, the city of New Orleans had been founded, the fabled river had been navigated by its first steamboat and the era had been born which Mark Twain was to chronicle so brilliantly.

Two years after Lewis and Clark traversed the Columbia to the Pacific, a young explorer named Simon Fraser embarked on a journey down a river which he mistakenly thought was the same Columbia. Born in Vermont, Fraser had signed on with the North West Company as a clerk in 1792. By 1801 he had been admitted as a partner and four years later he was assigned the entire district beyond the Rockies. In 1808, Fraser set out on a journey west, following the river first explored in 1793 by Alexander Mackenzie. He man-

Twilight descends purple and gold upon the Missouri River in South Dakota.

aged to survive a trip through the moiling Fraser River Canyon only to take bearings at the river's mouth and find, to his dismay, that the river could not possibly be the Columbia. He retraced his route.

David Thompson's travels and achievements are legendary. He began his career with the Hudson Bay Company and it was there that he learned the map-making and surveying skills for which he is justly famous. Ironically, the Company made little effort to put his surveying skills to good use, and, as a result, he quit in 1797 and joined the rival North West Company.

Within two years he had traveled over wide ranges of the Canadian and American west. His surveys included the Red River valley, part of the Missouri, the source of the Mississippi and the Rainy River area north of Lake Superior. Between 1806 and 1811 he surveyed west from the Saskatchewan and the Athabasca rivers and went on to map the entire length of the Columbia River.

Dry, rolling range, grazed by cattle, flanks the edges of the Little Missouri River in North Dakota. More national wildlife refuges grace this state than any other in the United States.

The Connecticut River near Sunderland, Massachusetts. Although Massachusetts is primarily an industrial state, it ranks first in the production of cranberries.

New Orleans, Louisiana, situated at the mouth of the Mississippi River, is a colorful city of early Spanish and French architecture reflecting the rich heritage of the Creole and Cajun people.

A man, panning for gold in Bonanza Creek near Dawson City, Yukon, is a ghostly reminder of the frenzied gold rush of 1898.

The Arkansas River, seen here from Petit Jean, Arkansas, serves as an industrial corridor reaching from Pine Bluff and Little Rock westward to Fort Smith.

PREVIOUS PAGES:

An empty log boom on the Rainy River at Fort Frances, Ontario, signals the passage of time. Booms were used to prevent the access of enemy ships and are now constructed to keep sawmill logs from floating away. The Rainy River flows from southern Ontario into Minnesota.

The waters of the Fraser River churn turquoise in Mount Robson Provincial Park, British Columbia.

Sunlight cuts through autumn fog at Phoca Rock, Columbia River as seen from Cape Horn, Washington.

The Green and Yampa rivers merge in the sullen, stormy setting of the Dinosaur National Monument, Utah.

Aitkin county, Minnesota. Coursing through forests of spruce, pine and birch, the Upper Mississippi River is not as fearsome here as in some other regions.

The Mississippi River in Minnesota, seen here beside gnarled trees and a crumbling shanty.

A canoe glides silently across the Ottawa River. Canada's Parliament Buildings are silhouetted in the distance.

A lone canoe is lodged on the shore of the eastern channel of the Mackenzie River at Inuvik, Northwest Territories.

As the pink and purple hues of sunset explode overhead, the mountains of Grand Teton National Park, Wyoming, embrace the Snake River.

The Rio Grande in Big Bend National Park, Texas, winds its way through a state of rugged mountains, dusty deserts and spectacular vistas.

A ridge of sand is built up by currents from the nearby Red Deer River in Alberta.

The Rainy River bridges the border between southern Ontario and northern Minnesota.

The mouth of the Klickitat River in the upper Columbia River Gorge, Washington. The basaltic lands of Oregon lie in the foreground.

Two routes run parallel, the railway line winding its way back in North American history to its creation in the late 1800s, and the Thompson River, Savona, British Columbia.

Weathered farmhouses and a sturdy chapel gaze out over the slate-colored waters of the St. Lawrence River in Port-au-Pérsil, Quebec.

The Mackenzie River curves its way beyond the continental tree line, north to the Arctic Ocean.

The Rio Grande gleams turquoise in this rugged New Mexico scene.

The Missouri River trails the North Dakota-Montana border in Big Sky Country.

Horse farms and endless rolling mountains frame the slow moving Susquehanna River in Rummerfield, Pennsylvania.

Itasca State Park in Minnesota boasts the headwaters of the Mississippi River.

Across the river from Niagara-on-the-Lake, Old Fort Niagara, New York, hugs the escarpment.

Indian Creek feeds water into the Buffalo National River, Arizona.

NEW
YORKER

2

COMMERCIAL RIVERS

BY THE TIME DAVID THOMPSON WAS MAPPING THE SASKATchewan, the Athabasca and the Columbia rivers in the early part of the nineteenth century, the fur trade was already on the wane. Though furs would remain the mainstay of North America's economy until the latter half of the century, the trappers and traders were wearing out their welcome with their avarice and their gross miscalculation of the extent of North America's animal wealth.

The continent was undergoing dramatic changes. Increasingly, native North Americans were being disenfranchised—pushed to the fringes and forced to live on reservations—while the lands which had been theirs for millennia were being claimed by the pioneers pushing westward.

As the forests were felled and the lands tilled, the rivers of North America came to have new importance. Where once they had been traversed, and relatively seldom, by native peoples, explorers and voyageurs, rivers

As the Hudson River flows in the forefront, the Empire State Building in downtown Manhattan touches the sky.

were becoming the highways of steamships and tugs. These vessels brought trade goods inland, and carried the products of farms to distant markets. In the era before the construction of roads, rivers were truly the highways of the new land.

Without them, the history and the development of Canada and the United States would have been markedly different. Rivers permitted exploration of the interior of the continent, and it was along these rivers that forts and trading posts were constructed. Most of them were to become the focal point for the great river cities of today: New York, Albany, Pittsburgh, Philadelphia, Detroit, Cincinnati, Omaha, Memphis and New Orleans—to name but a few in the United States; Saint John, Quebec, Montreal, Ottawa, Windsor, Winnipeg, Edmonton and Vancouver, among many others in Canada.

Of all the North American rivers, the St. Lawrence is unquestionably the most important. Curiously enough, it is far from the longest: from its source, the eastern end of Lake Ontario, to its outlet at the Gulf of St. Lawrence, the river measures only 800 miles. Together with its tributaries—the Saguenay, the Ottawa, the St. Maurice, the Richelieu, the Manicouagan—and the Great Lakes themselves, it allows access to a vast area of northern and central Canada and the northeastern United States.

It was by following the St. Lawrence and by navigating the Great Lakes that explorers gained access to the Mississippi and, as a result, to an equally vast area in what is now the central and western United States. In terms of today's trade and transportation, the St. Lawrence truly is, as Cartier described it, "the great river of Canada" and could just as aptly be named, along with the Mississippi, the great highway of North America.

Before the invasion of European colonials, the natives of North America were well acquainted with the St. Lawrence and made ample use of it. As a major river artery, the St. Lawrence allowed the tribes not only to trade with each other but to move with ease from one hunting ground to another, and it was for these purposes that they created a craft ideally suited to the environment and their needs: the canoe. The Europeans, unable to sail past the rapids of the major rivers like the St. Lawrence, and stymied by the portages required to skirt the boiling waters of many of the major trading rivers, were forced to abandon sailboats and adopt the canoe in order to gain access to the fur-trading tribes of the interior.

Limited to these relatively small craft, European traders had to paddle and portage into the heart of the country, carrying awkward packs filled with the wares they wanted to trade for pelts, and making the return trip—often weeks, sometimes months, in duration—back to the trading posts along the shores of the Great Lakes or the banks of the great rivers.

It was a time-consuming process and far from profitable; it was not long before the Europeans devised a better method. Rather than have one crew go all the way inland in order to trade with the Indian people, trips were arranged in stages, with different crews. Trade goods were brought inland from New York and Montreal and left at trading posts. These crews would then take bundles of pelts back to the major cities. Meanwhile, the traders would pick up the goods and move further inland, negotiate their deals and return to the supply depots. It involved twice the manpower, but it also doubled the speed and efficiency of the operation. And it left us, today, with the legacy of communities which have sprung up around these early posts.

A riverboat's spinning red wheel churns the waters of the Mississippi River.

The rapids and waterfalls of North America's rivers bedevilled explorers and traders alike during the early exploration and trading years. Obstructions such as these were problematic and offered no easy solution. The Sulpician monks serving at Montreal toward the end of the seventeenth century came up with a bright idea: digging by hand, they created a canal a few feet deep by a dozen wide to skirt the Lachine rapids. However unsophisticated in execution, the principle of that canal could not have been more sound. It was the beginning of a series of locks and canals which ultimately led to the construction of the St. Lawrence Seaway—a system which once and for all opened North America to business.

That business boom has been prospering ever since the Seaway was officially opened in 1959. Seven locks were constructed upriver from Montreal, another eight form the Welland Canal which allows ships to bypass the spectacularly unnavigable Niagara and make passage between lakes Ontario and Erie. Together with the St. Mary's River Canal, which gives entry to Lake Superior, this system of locks and canals permits oceangoing freighters to dock in the very heart of the North American continent. It has created what has been described as the greatest inland waterway in the world.

Unfortunately, the Seaway was bitterly opposed by officials and politicians in ports all along the Eastern Seaboard and by the owners and managers of railways: they perceived the system as a threat to their own privileged and profitable position. These eastern barons and businessmen argued, without effect, that it would constitute an unwarranted government subsidy for the owners of marine shipping firms.

Their concerns were not without foundation. The Seaway has led to an almost fivefold increase in the quantities of goods shipped through the St. Lawrence River section of the Seaway, and has created stiff competition in the shipments of grain from the west, lumber from the north, steel from the mills of Pennsylvania and Ontario, and manufactured goods both inward and outward bound. The initial cost of $460 million—$330 million of it paid by Canada—seems a bargain by today's standards.

Far to the north and the west there is another great river system. Though the Mackenzie River itself is only 900 miles in length, from Great Slave Lake to the Beaufort Sea, its system of tributaries is massive. From its most distant beginning, the Athabasca River in northern Alberta, the river system stretches more than 2,600 miles to the Arctic. In North America, only the Mississippi is longer.

The Mackenzie system drains nearly three quarters of a million square miles: vast regions of the Northwest Territories as well as the northern edges of British Columbia, Alberta and Saskatchewan.

By 1820, trading forts had been established at various posts along the river, mainly at the river junctions, to take advantage of trade with Indian tribes who lived further inland. By the mid 1820s, canoes had been abandoned in favor of York boats which could carry as much as three tons of furs. It was not until the closing years of the nineteenth century that steam-powered vessels began plying the river. As on the Mississippi, far to the south, paddle wheelers were popular on the Mackenzie, but these days the river's settlements and worksites are serviced by tugboats and barges during the relatively brief ice-free shipping season.

Though the Mackenzie region is sparsely populated and, for vast tracts, absolutely unspoiled, it has been and continues to be the subject of intense developmental interest. Gold rushes have given way to the mining of minerals and metals and the Mackenzie's future will undoubtedly hinge on the ability of multinational corporations to win approval for oil and gas exploration and transshipment.

There are considerable oil and gas deposits in both the Beaufort Sea, to the north, and in the tar sands of the Athabasca region to the south. So delicate is the environment, and so intense the concern about the harmful effects of development—particularly in the oil fields—that the Canadian government was forced to appoint a federal Royal Commission to examine the arguments for and against a pipeline to bring gas down the Mackenzie Valley to Alberta. Judge Thomas Berger, chairman of the commission, could not have been clearer: under no circumstances should the government allow a pipeline to be constructed across the tundra.

Oil and gas exploration are not the only concerns in the far north. The possibility of tapping both the Mackenzie and, farther west, the Yukon, have met with considerable opposition. Some hydroelectric facilities have been constructed on tributaries of the Mackenzie and on the Yukon at Miles Canyon. Though the benefits of further development are obvious to some, the drawbacks are equally obvious to others.

Further east, the mighty Nelson has been harnessed at three sites to provide hydroelectric power. No wonder: its outflow at Hudson Bay is roughly equal to that of the Columbia. The Nelson was an integral route in the fur trade during the seventeenth century for, turbulent though it was, the river still cut the shortest route from Hudson Bay to Lake Winnipeg, and it was in hopes of using this northern route that the Hudson Bay Company built two forts near its mouth by the latter part of this same century.

By the late nineteenth century, western farmers made some attempt to use the Nelson to send their wheat to Hudson Bay and from there to European markets. A railway was eventually built alongside the Nelson, connecting the interior to Churchill, Manitoba.

When nickel was discovered near the site of present-day Thompson, in 1956, a new use was soon found for the Nelson. Because of its steep drop and massive volume—it is the outlet for the Saskatchewan River system—it was an ideal source of hydro power. Since then, three hydroelectric projects have been completed and together they provide ample power for the nickel smelters at Thompson.

Like its vast Canadian cousin the Mackenzie, the American Mississippi and its main tributary, the Missouri, serve to drain more than one million square miles in the American mid-west—one-eighth of the land mass of North America.

The raging Missouri could not have been a more obvious source of hydroelectricity. There are four major hydro dams on the Missouri— including the controversial Garrison Dam in North Dakota—and together they provide flood control, electricity and irrigation for an area of about five million acres.

The Mississippi, like the St. Lawrence, has been a major water highway since earliest times. During the years when the fur trade was burgeoning, voyageurs and traders penetrated lands where they made contact with the tribes as far west as the Rockies and as far east as the Appalachians.

When the fur trade fell into decline and entrepreneurs turned their attention first to lumbering, and then to mining, in the far north of Minnesota, the Mississippi became a busy watercourse. During the last century, great rafts of logs were floated down from the northern forests to mills downstream in Minneapolis. The stern-wheelers, which are the signature of the age which Mark Twain immortalized in his prose, made possible the expansion of settlement in the west. Settlers gained access, by the Mississippi and her tributaries, to their new homes in the west and relied on those steamers to bring the trade goods which they required and to transport their crops to market.

Though the Mississippi was upstaged, for some time, by both rail and highway transportation, it remains today one of the world's busiest waterways. Despite the treacheries of low water and shifting sandbanks, the river is still a major transportation route for all manner of goods—from the grain of the prairie west to the coal from mountain mines. The cities which line its banks have been celebrated in literature and song. They are among the most well-known in the United States: Minneapolis-St. Paul in Minnesota, Dubuque in Iowa, Burlington in Vermont, St. Louis in Missouri, Memphis in Tennessee, Baton Rouge and New Orleans in Louisiana.

The river has been an irascible mistress. Great floods in the early part of this century wreaked havoc, created damage estimated in the millions of dollars and left hundreds of thousands homeless. The problem is most acute when spring rains swell the Ohio in the east, and sudden mild temperatures result in massive melting of snows in the west. When those waters meet the Mississippi, disaster is inevitable. As a result of such flooding, the U.S. Corps of Engineers constructed a series of artificial levees which allow the diversion of floodwaters into several low-lying areas designated for these purposes.

Flood control is not the only modern wonder of the Mississippi. A canal was constructed at Chicago creating a link between the Great Lakes and the Mississippi, via the Illinois River, and so it is possible to navigate in this century, as it was not in the last, all the way from the Gulf of Mexico to the Gulf of St. Lawrence.

It was this route, though by portage rather than by canal, which the earliest explorers had followed in search of a New World. Retracing their route, from the Gulf of Mexico to the great northern gulf, one can not help but be struck by the great diversities of people and communities who take their living from the land on the banks of this great river. The explorers would be bewildered, indeed, if they followed the Mississippi to the end of all its possibilities.

They would be equally confused if they veered east at Cairo, Illinois and ventured up the Ohio River. Following this route, they would pass through places like Wheeling, West Virginia, Louisville, Kentucky, Cincinatti, Ohio and Pittsburgh, Pennsylvania, and would find themselves in the very heartland of American industry and commerce.

If, just east of Cairo, they followed the Tennessee River instead, they would perhaps be even more bewildered. The Tennessee was first navigated by steamboat in 1828. A century later, work had begun which would turn the Tennessee into a textbook example of what can be done to harness a river's power to human needs.

The arch above St. Louis, Missouri, a city that straddles two great rivers, makes this historic river city unmistakable.

Long, swift and prone to flooding, the Tennessee was also a natural and tempting source of hydroelectric power. In the middle 1930s, the Tennessee Valley Authority was created and in the intervening half century, the T.V.A. has spawned a system of locks and dams to aid navigation, control flooding and harness the river's vast power. Its power utilities produce more than three million kilowatts of electricity. Thanks to the locks, the Tennessee is a major route of shipment for goods which range from automobiles to fertilizer.

But the Authority's expertise has grown far beyond those areas of concern. It has become known around the world, in fact, for its progress in the areas of regional planning and development, soil conservation, wildlife preservation and outdoor education.

Far to the west, on the Columbia River, experts were equally quick to see the potential of a vast river system. Running 1,200 miles from the Rocky Mountains through British Columbia and the states of Washington and Oregon, and emptying into the Pacific, the river now features some of the most massive hydroelectric dams in the world.

These projects are unique in that they are the work of Canada and the United States and were undertaken under the auspices of the Columbia River Treaty. The treaty was not signed, and the work undertaken, without controversy and opposition. In order to harness the river, considerable environmental damage had to be done and there were those who felt the benefits—in either power or revenue—would not be worth the loss of land and forest in the flooded areas. There was also considerable concern for the salmon which annually arrived far upriver in some of the largest spawning beds to be found anywhere in the world. Despite the protests—and at considerable cost in terms of lost land and damage to the spawning grounds—the projects went ahead and its dams, including the Grand Coulee, are now among the largest in the world.

Certain rivers are a blessing to farmers, and the Rio Grande has been such a blessing since before the "discoverers" arrived in the New World from the Old. Long before the Spanish arrived in the first half of the sixteenth century, native peoples have been using the waters of the Rio Grande to irrigate their fields.

Little has changed. What was once accomplished by hand, has now been replaced with sophisticated machines. The result is a series of massive dams and canals. Elephant Butte, for example, near the town of Truth or Consequences, New Mexico is an impressive dam. More than 300 feet high and 1,600 across, it is part of the Rio Grande Project whose triple goals are hydroelectric power, flood control and irrigation.

The Rio Grande is central to the economies—and the legends—of a host of communities whose names are known through story and song: Albuquerque, El Paso and Laredo. Since the end of the Mexican War in the middle of the nineteenth century, the river has served as the boundary between the United States and Mexico.

Like the mighty St. Lawrence far to the north, it serves as a reminder of who we are, and who we are not.

OPPOSITE PAGE:

The turbulent Rio Grande carves its way through Texas and New Mexico, hugging a landscape of rugged mountains, sweeping grasslands and dusty deserts.

The lights of Williamsport, Pennsylvania, glimmer within a rose-tinged landscape. Lycoming County's Susquehanna River flows past Amish and Mennonite communities.

An aerial photograph taken from St. Louis, Missouri frames the rolling fields of Mississippi farmland.

Rows of houses line the banks of the Grande River in Quebec.

Hydro water channels divert water from the Niagara River toward its generating station, producing hydroelectric power.

The R. Moses Power complex along the Niagara River in New York is a powerful source of hydroelectricity.

Grand Coulee Dam, Washington. The Columbia River, which flows for nearly 1,200 miles through British Columbia, Washington and Oregon, empties into the Pacific Ocean off the coast of Oregon.

OVERLEAF:

The International Bridge over the St. Lawrence River joins Cornwall, Ontario, to Hogansburg, New York. The river, at this juncture, is extremely narrow.

The American Falls surges out of Lake Erie and marks the boundary between Canada and the United States. Its waters eventually roll past Buffalo and spill into Lake Ontario.

The Niagara River in Ontario thunders into Niagara Falls, its movement frozen by the cold snap of a North American winter.

This quaint opening signals the start of the longest-covered bridge in the world and is found in Hartland, New Brunswick, crossing the St. John River.

Strung with strips of steel, the Brooklyn Bridge crosses the East River and frames Manhattan, New York.

The California Aqueduct. Irrigated farms in arid California are scientific marvels, transforming desert valleys into lush fields of fruit and vegetables.

Framed by successive bridges, the Susquehanna River washes slate-grey through Pennsylvania's capital city, Harrisburg.

The Charles River in Cambridge, Massachusetts, flows meditatively past this university town.

A fisherman is silhouetted against the Connecticut River.

The Chicago River runs gray beneath downstate Chicago, Illinois. Chicago is a major Great Lakes port, trading by barge on the Illinois Waterway to the Mississippi, by ship with other lake ports and overseas by means of the St. Lawrence Seaway.

The Detroit River, which empties into Lake Erie, laps the edge of Detroit, Michigan.

Its city lights iridescent in the night, Detroit as seen from Windsor, Ontario by rail ferry.

Two Mississippi riverboats approach St. Louis, Missouri.

Its wheel churning the waters of the St. Lawrence River, a ferry carries a boatload of tourists into the circle of the Thousand Islands at the mouth of Lake Ontario.

A transport truck races past the Suwannee River in Florida. First in citrus produce, Florida is second only to California in the growth of vegetables.

Boston, Massachusetts. An aerial view over Harvard University and the Charles River extends to the city center.

A concrete bridge, thrust over the Genesee River, follows the line of downtown Rochester, New York.

The architecture of downtown Rochester, New York, is mirrored in the still waters of the Genesee River.

Dusk sweeps the Victoria pier in Montreal, Quebec.

Lush coastal mountains near Portland, Oregon, embrace the Columbia River gorge. As much as 200 inches of precipitation a year falls near the west coast, while less than 8 inches reaches eastern Oregon.

Thousand Islands, New York. Boldt Castle is framed by reeds along the St. Lawrence shoreline.

The Long Sault Parkway on the southern shores of Ontario, and the Long Sault Spillway Dam, bridging Ontario and New York, were carved out after the construction of the St. Lawrence Seaway.

A windswept view of the Thousand Islands from the American Thousand Islands bridge.

Saint Johns River houseboats motor along the only river in Florida to flow north and south.

The Columbia River near Portland, Oregon. The leading state in timber production, Oregon yields more than a fourth of the softwood lumber grown in the United States.

Built in the midst of Arizona's blue-sky land of saguaro deserts and red cliffs, the Hoover Dam taps Colorado River water from below the Grand Canyon and channels it as far east as Tucson, Arizona.

The TransCanada Highway 1 runs parallel, for a time, to the St. John River in New Brunswick.

A Mississippi River barge, making its way from Mississippi to Missouri, may contain lumber, soybeans or cotton.

The Potomac river stretches darkly into an amber horizon in Virginia.

While the East River glimmers in the foreground, the United Nations building, New York, is reflected in the United Nations Plaza Hotel.

3

WILDERNESS RIVERS

THE ST. LAWRENCE, THE NIAGARA, THE DETROIT, THE RIO GRANDE—all these border rivers do, indeed, suggest who we are not. But the obverse also holds true: there are certain rivers which reflect something of who we are.

We North Americans are, curiously, still a wilderness people. Though collectively we seem to have done our best to obliterate the last vestiges of nature in the cities where most of us live, and though a great many of us never wander farther from the beaten path than the paved walkway through a city park, there lingers within many of us a romantic attachment to nature. For hundreds of thousands of us in Canada and the United States, the call of the wild may be a weak call and an intermittent one; it is a compelling call nonetheless.

We deem it important—some would say essential—to send our children to camp each summer so they may learn something of the joy of being

Brilliant red and white sandstone in the cliffs of the Grand Canyon preserve an entanglement of Precambrian fossils. These cliffs rise above the Colorado River.

surrounded not by buildings, but by trees, so they may discover something of the thrill and terror involved in swimming in water which is deep beyond diving, and so they may come to savor the solitude which Henry Thoreau, author of *Walden*, so rightly and highly prized.

We value all this ourselves, however fitfully. Stand on the shoulder of the road on the outskirts of the city—any city, any weekend—and you will need a calculator to count the mobile homes, the trailers and the campers which make their way toward cottage country and camping grounds. For all such sojourners, summer would not be summer unless at least a weekend of it was spent on the shore of a lake, or on the bank of a river, lulled by the wind in the trees and the calls and cries of the birds in the air.

Is there one of us who, sitting on such a shore or riverbank, has not dreamt of chucking it all and hying off to some distant wooded place, there to carve out a new and a cleaner and less complicated life? Is there one of us who would not quietly claim to be perfectly capable of living far from the din of urban life?

Would any picture of such a perfect imagined wilderness Eden be complete without a river rushing for the lake or the sea, its urgent voice obliterating all other sounds, and most of our earthly worries as well?

The South Nahanni River, in Canada's Northwest Territories, would qualify admirably on anyone's list of wilderness Edens. It is the heart of one of Canada's most spectacular national parks—the park itself is a World Heritage Site—and if one were to attempt to define the term wilderness river, the South Nahanni would be a good starting point. This furious river rages through canyons, each of which is more than 3,000 feet in depth, and finally hurtles over the 300-foot Virginia Falls.

In the early part of this century, fortune seekers tripped over themselves to get to the region, lured by tales of abandoned gold mines. Some of these prospectors were never seen again. The region is rife with speculation as to the fates of more than two dozen men.

These days, a different breed of adventurer is lured to the river in the southwest corner of the Northwest Territories. The park is a magnet for canoeists and wilderness campers who are drawn as much by an opportunity for spiritual renewal as by the desire to push themselves to the limits of their wilderness abilities. They are treated, in a splendid natural sideshow, to displays of plant life and to glimpses of animal life that they are hard pressed to match anywhere else. There are more than one hundred species of birds in the area—including eagles and falcons—and more than thirty species of animals—including caribou and grizzly bears.

As important as national parks are for their human visitors, they serve another function: they are vast tracts of land set aside for the use and protection of the animals and birds which roam them, and the plants and trees which thrive in them. Large as they are, these parks are the last refuge for all manner of animals and birds—from grizzly bears and falcons, to caribou and eagles—which have been driven nearly to the brink of extinction by man's relentless drive for progress.

The South Nahanni is one of a number of northern rivers which serve as tributaries for the magnificent Mackenzie. For the four or five months of the year when it is ice free, the Mackenzie is surely one of the most beautiful of

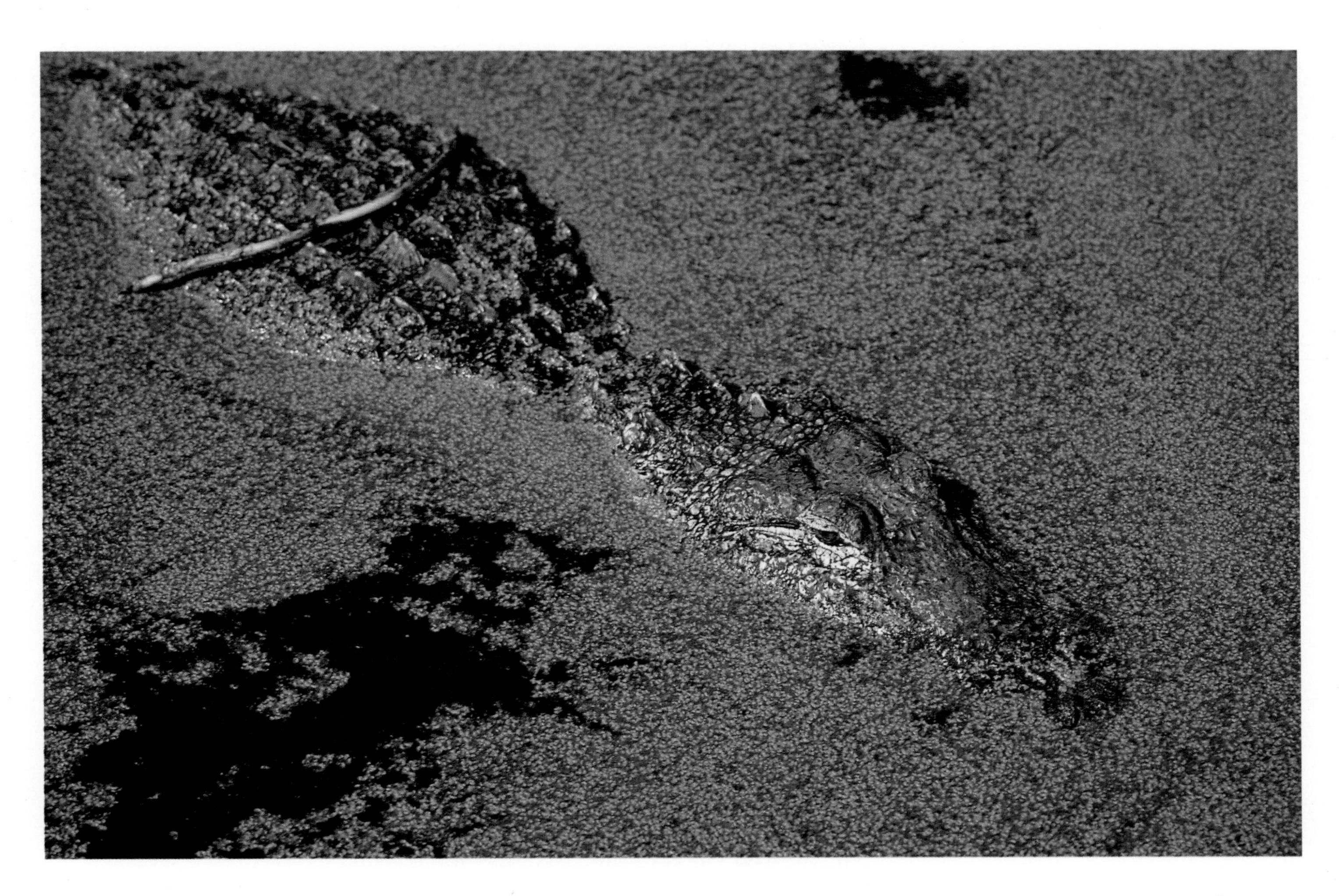

With one eye staring darkly, an alligator emerges from the algae-smeared waters of the Mississippi River.

Canada's rivers. Traversing and draining the entire Northwest Territories, and shadowed on the west by the Mackenzie Mountain range, the Mackenzie is a breathtaking river route throughout the northwest.

Along its course, the Mackenzie is joined by its tributaries, such as the Liard, Nahanni, Keele and Peel flowing in from the west and the Willowlake, Great Bear and Hare Indian from the east. As with any river of such a length, the Mackenzie changes dramatically in mood. In some places where the terrain is relatively flat, it appears to be a wide and lazy northern version of the Mississippi. In other places, it torrents through canyons and is all but unnavigable.

Any one of the Mackenzie's tributaries would be more than enough to occupy the most demanding of wilderness canoeists. The Liard—which takes its name not from an explorer, but from a poplar to be found all along its length—is a good example.

Once a section of the northern fur trade route, the Liard is a wild and unforgiving river. Past Fort Liard, a couple of hundred miles from the river's confluence with the Mackenzie, even the most hardy and adventurous of travelers is forced ashore.

The Peace River, another of its tributaries, is perhaps more famous. Flowing down out of the Rockies and then east and north, the Peace eventually empties into the Slave River and thus feeds the mighty Mackenzie.

Farther north and east, straddling the Alberta-Northwest Territories border is Wood Buffalo National Park, Canada's largest park region. Wood Buffalo was established as a sanctuary for its threatened namesake, and is now a sanctuary for all manner of northern wildlife and waterfowl: western woodland caribou, whooping cranes, peregrine falcons, Cooper's hawks and great gray owls, to name but a few. It is a sanctuary and a home as well to those whose ancestors have lived here for millennia: Cree, Chipewyan and Beaver Indians. And Wood Buffalo has become a favored spot for those who seek to get as far as possible, for however brief a time, from the city.

To the west of the Mackenzie, the Yukon River runs nearly two thousand miles from the confluence of the Pelly and Lewes rivers in British Columbia all the way through the Yukon Territory and Alaska to the Bering Sea. If you are looking for wildlife, look no farther. Vast areas of the Yukon's drainage basin have been declared wildlife refuges. One of them, the Yukon Flats National Wildlife Refuge in northern Alaska, encompasses an area of two and a half million acres.

The variety of wildlife is both astonishing and heartening. Here in the far north, relatively safe from the reach of modern man, all manner of mammals and more than one hundred species of birds have found a place to raise their young. The Yukon is a veritable canoeist's delight: on any given day you might be rewarded with the sight of a moose raising its muzzle from the water near the shore, the ineffable call of a sandhill crane, the soaring ascent of a whistling swan, or the sight of a grizzly raising her snout to the wind before sauntering off in search of lunch.

Far to the east lie a number of rivers which exercise a strong pull on canoeists and hikers. The Kazan is high on that list. It is not a long river, but it is a challenging and popular one among canoeists. Cutting across the southeastern portion of the Northwest Territories from the Saskatchewan border, it gives access to the Thelon River, farther north and east. The Thelon's other main tributary, the Dubawnt River, flows from Dubawnt Lake, and the Thelon itself flows north and east draining in Hudson Bay.

This whole area was once home to massive herds of caribou which numbered in the hundreds of thousands. The depletion of the caribou is one of the sorrowful notes sounded in the history of Canada's north. The caribou, like the buffalo farther south, were once the signature of this wild country. The abandon with which hunters pursued and slaughtered them is astonishing. It is difficult to imagine such massive herds reduced to so few by relatively small groups of well-armed hunters. It was to prevent the massacre of another of the north's great species—the muskox—that a large part of the Thelon territory was declared a game sanctuary in 1927.

It is ironic that the man who recommended the creation of the sanctuary two years earlier, died the year it was created. John Hornby and two companions starved to death in a cabin on the banks of the Thelon between Great Slave Lake and Chesterfield Inlet on Hudson Bay. Hornby, Harold Adlard and Edgar Christian had come north to test themselves against the elements and to live as best they could on the resources of the land. They gambled then on the migration of the caribou. But the caribou, that year, chose to move by another route. And in the silence of that long wintry wait, the three died, one by one, their story captured in Christian's published diary, *Death in the Barren Ground.*

Some of the most spectacular of Canada's rivers are obviously to be found in the mountains. Unhappily for adventurers, they are also the most inaccessible. The Fraser is an exception. Cascading through the Rockies of British Columbia, the Fraser River has been seen and photographed by hundreds of thousands of tourists. When gold was found in these fabulous hills in the middle of the nineteenth century, the prospectors were quick to create a route of access. They managed to carve a thin trail into the side of the mountains—the Caribou Road—and when the railway men were trying to figure out how to lay a roadbed through the mountains, they concluded that the easiest and cheapest route would be to follow the Thompson and Fraser rivers.

As a result the most unadventurous of visitors can now look down from a railway car window into the furious river below. The vista is most impressive at Hell's Gate, south of the community of Lytton. Here, as the train inches along its twisting line, the traveler will find himself three thousand feet above the turgid waters of the river. Seen in the middle of the night, under full moonlight, it is a vista not soon erased from memory. Just as unforgettable, in their own way, are the lush and majestic rain forests which tower over the banks of the Fraser at its delta.

Canada has its share of majestic rivers, but certainly has no monopoly on them. In one case, Canada and the United States have combined to protect waterways. Though not strictly speaking a river, the famed boundary waters which separate Minnesota and Ontario and connect Lake Superior with Lake Winnipeg have been declared a kind of gigantic international park. On the American side, more than one million acres of northern Minnesota have been declared the Boundary Waters Canoe Area. On the Ontario side, an equally vast area has been transformed into Quetico Provincial Park. There are more than twelve hundred miles of canoe trails in the combined wilderness areas. Although many of these trails are a canoeist's delight, many more miles are anything but. After portaging for half a dozen miles with canoes and supplies, the modern-day outdoors adventurer will have gained an entirely new respect for the voyageurs who traveled this way once and thought nothing of jogging six or eight miles while carrying a pack weighing almost two hundred pounds, and repeating that trip three or four times until a portage was completed.

Some of the wildest of the continent's wilderness rivers are to be found in the mountains of the northwest United States. Two among them bear special mention.

The Snake River has a well-deserved reputation for being the match of most outdoors adventurers. Its famed Hell's Canyon is, indeed, more than aptly named. The canyon is in excess of 120 miles in length and, for one forty-mile stretch, its average depth is more than 5,000 feet. At one spot it is nearly 8,000 feet deep and earns its title as the continent's deepest canyon. Shouldered by mountains, its waters raging through constrictions of sheer rock, it has taken its toll among the foolish and the ill-prepared.

Flowing down from the mountains to the east, and eventually serving as a tributary to the Snake, is the notorious Salmon River—the river which once was known as the river-of-no-return. The Salmon proved all too difficult for Meriwether Lewis and William Clark. Daunted by the rapids and the impossibility of portaging its almost vertical banks, the explorers turned back and eventually made their way to the Pacific by another, and less formidable, route. Its canyons, in places deeper than the Grand Canyon, are littered with the bones of the boats of men who overestimated their skill, or ran out of luck. Though today many come to the Salmon—there are rafting trips down the river—extreme caution is well advised.

Like the Fraser far to the north, the Colorado River is probably one of the most renowned rivers in the world. But the vast majority of these visitors do their gazing and daydreaming from high on the lips of the Marble and Grand Canyons, or from the relative safety of the riverbanks.

Thundering over more than one hundred rapids into the world's most famous canyon, the Colorado is born high in the mountains of Wyoming and empties eventually into the Gulf of California. It is a formidable and a dangerous river, and it is not by accident that you can travel most of its 1,700-mile length and see no human settlement.

The Rio Grande, tumbling down out of the mountains of Colorado, courses through some of the most beautiful country in the United States. An avid canoeist will find it all but impossible to select one section of the 1,880-mile river as more beautiful than another but the terrain between Presidio and Langtry, part of which comprises Big Bend National Park, is a favorite with many of those familiar with the river.

It would be easy to write on and on of the wilderness rivers of this vast continent of ours. Those rivers which have been mentioned are but a few among the vast number which course through our countries, and our lives. Each, for those who have traveled upon them, holds a special place in the imagination, shaping both our perceptions and the way we define ourselves. It is still possible, for example, to stand in a certain wild spot and see a river flowing much the same way as it flowed past the feet of our North American ancestors.

Of course, the passage of time has altered our rivers in certain ways. It is frightening to contemplate the mix of chemicals and pollutants which have

combined together, in lethal doses and variations, to poison our waters, killing fish and nearby wildlife in the process.

It is worth remembering that, long after we are gone, these rivers will still run to distant seas, and that our daughters and sons will want to stand on the banks, as we have done, transfixed by the magic of a river's music and lulled by its flow.

They deserve their inheritance. Their children do, as well.

Snow-covered peaks surround the Kootenay River in Kootenay National Park, British Columbia.

Canoeists are suspended in the evening light upon the Snake River, Grand Teton National Park, Wyoming.

Deer Creek Falls plunges from chiselled rock in the Grand Canyon, Arizona.

Two boaters appear overwhelmed by the monstrous pinnacles, temples and hoodoos of the Grand Canyon.

A sojourner in Anasazi Cave is given a rare view of the Grand Canyon, its multilayered rock carved out hundreds of millions of years ago.

The Coppermine River, which courses north of the continental tree line, crosses both treeless tundra and forest regions in the Northwest Territories.

The Gibbon River in Yellowstone National Park, Wyoming, flows past towering conifers and jagged mountain peaks. Energy-rich Wyoming boasts natural resources of oil, coal and uranium as well as unspoiled wilderness preserves.

The Shoshone River winds its way past spectacular rock near Cody, Wyoming.

Low water on Wanapitei River, Ontario, flows miles north of Lake Huron.

The Shoshone River near Cody, Wyoming. Cowboys and rodeos flourish in this arid, energy-rich state.

In Colorado, just south of the 40th parallel, the Black Canyon of the Gunnison National Monument is carved into the landscape.

Oneonta Falls spills from the lush coastal mountains of the Columbia River Gorge, Oregon.

PREVIOUS PAGES:

A northern mountain range, rising out of Jasper National Park, Alberta, is mirrored in the translucent waters of the Athabasca River.

Mount Moran, Wyoming, seen among the Teton Mountains, rises above the Snake River, one of the many wilderness rivers found in this lofty Rocky Mountain state.

The Colorado River carves the Glenwood Canyon into sharply mirrored halves.

The pristine waters of Takakkaw Falls plunge into the Yoho River in Yoho National Park, British Columbia.

Teeming with trout, the Black River rushes through Wisconsin's lake-spangled northern woods, cascading, at points, into waterfalls.

Mammoth Cave National Park, Kentucky. An eerie, emerald opacity lends Green River its name.

Moose Park, Northwest Territories. Mist veils Mount Wilson as the waters of the Nahanni River lap reeds.

Mountain meltwater runs from the coastal ranges that surround Glacier Bay, Alaska.

PHOTOGRAPH CREDITS

Gene Ahrens, *Superstock/Four By Five*, 17

Tom Algire/*Tom Stack & Associates*, 109

Craig Aurness/*First Light Associated Photographers*, 69

Mike Beedell, 5, 28, 92, 101, 102, 103, 104

Annie Griffiths Belt/*First Light Associated Photographers*, 51, 74

Matt Bradley/*Tom Stack & Associates*, 31

Fraser Clark, 3, 9, 88, 118

Tom Coker, *Superstock/Four By Five*, 22

W. Perry Conway/*Tom Stack & Associates*, 30

John de Visser, 19, 20-21, 32, 33, 34, 36, 37, 42, 56, 57, 58, 60-61, 62, 63, 64, 65, 72, 73, 75, 78, 79, 81, 82, 83, 84, 90

Terry Donnelly/*Tom Stack & Associates*, 43

Stewart M. Green/*Tom Stack & Associates*, 66

Roger N.J. Hostin, 23, 99, 110-111, 115

R. King, *Superstock/Four By Five*, 53

Robert Landau/*First Light Associated Photographers*, 55

Larry Lee/*First Light Associated Photographers*, 89

R.A. Lee, *Superstock/Four By Five*, 67

R. Llewellyn, *Superstock/Four By Five*, 91

Sandy MacDonald, 29, 116

Michael Philip Manheim/*First Light Associated Photographers*, 6

Don McPhee, 59

Gary Milburn/*Tom Stack & Associates*, 15

Brian Milne/*First Light Associated Photographers*, 24, 119

Warren Morgan/*First Light Associated Photographers*, 80

Scott Nielsen, 26, 41, 117

Timothy O'Keefe/*Tom Stack & Associates*, 85

Brian Parker/*Tom Stack & Associates*, 95

Jessie Parker/*First Light Associated Photographers*, 18, 27

Milton Rand/*Tom Stack & Associates*, 13, 25, 35

Bob Sell/*Tom Stack & Associates*, 47

Shostal, *Superstock/Four By Five*, 76, 87, 113

Richard Simpson, 106

Doug Sokell/*Tom Stack & Associates*, 112

Steve Strickland/*First Light Associated Photographers*, 54

W. Strode, *Superstock/Four By Five*, 1

Superstock/*Four By Five*, 40, 70, 77, 105

Jack D. Swenson/*Tom Stack & Associates*, 100

E. Van Hoorick, *Superstock/Four By Five*, 16

Dudley Witney, 38, 39, 68, 71, 86, 107, 108, 114

Mike Yamashita/*First Light Associated Photographers*, 44